Thanksgiving

By David F. Marx

Consultant
Katharine A. Kane, Reading Specialist
Former Language Arts Coordinator
San Diego County Office of Education

⊄P Children's Press®
A Division of Grolier Publishing
New York   London   Hong Kong   Sydney
Danbury, Connecticut

Visit Children's Press® on the Internet at:
http://publishing.grolier.com

Designer: Herman Adler Design Group
Photo Researcher: Caroline Anderson

Library of Congress Cataloging-in-Publication Data

Marx, David F.
    Thanksgiving / by David F. Marx.
        p. cm — (Rookie read-about holidays)
    Includes index.
    Summary: Introduces the history, customs, meaning, and celebration of
Thanksgiving.
        ISBN 0-516-22208-2 (lib. bdg.)   0-516-27157-1 (pbk.)
        1. Thanksgiving Day—Juvenile literature. 2. Harvest festivals—Juvenile
literature. [1. Thanksgiving Day. 2. Holidays.] I. Title.
    GT4975.M37   2000
    394.2649—dc21   00-022634

Do you celebrate
Thanksgiving?

November 2000

Sunday	Monday	Tuesday	Wednesday	Thursday	Friday	Saturday
			1	2	3	4
5	6	7	8	9	10	11
12	13	14	15	16	17	18
19	20	21	22	**23**	24	25
26	27	28	29	30		

In the United States, people celebrate Thanksgiving on the fourth Thursday of November.

October 2000

Sunday	Monday	Tuesday	Wednesday	Thursday	Friday	Saturday
1	2	3	4	5	6	7
8	9	10	11	12	13	14
15	16	17	18	19	20	21
22	23	24	25	26	27	28
29	30	31				

In Canada, Thanksgiving is on the second Monday in October.

For many years in many lands, people have had holidays to give thanks for a good harvest.

A harvest is when farmers go to their fields and collect all the food they have grown.

Harvesting corn

An ancient harvest celebration

Harvest holidays took place way back in ancient times—in Greece, Rome, Egypt, and China.

In America, the big harvest holiday is Thanksgiving. The first American Thanksgiving was celebrated in 1621.

The first Thanksgiving

The Pilgrims land in America.

In the 1600s, people started coming to America from Europe, a land across the Atlantic Ocean. The first group of newcomers was called the Pilgrims.

The Pilgrims built small towns and planted farms.

Native Americans already lived there. They helped the Pilgrims grow new foods.

The Pilgrims invited Native Americans to the first Thanksgiving.

The Pilgrims and Native Americans

Today, nobody really knows if turkey was eaten at the first American Thanksgiving. We do know the meal included deer, oysters, boiled pumpkin, corn, and cranberries.

Oysters

Pumpkins

Cranberries

Do you have a big turkey dinner on Thanksgiving? Today, almost everyone eats turkey on this holiday.

Wild turkeys

Some people call it
"Turkey Day!"

What other foods do you
eat at Thanksgiving?

Sweet potatoes? Stuffing?
Pumpkin pie? Every family
has its own favorite
Thanksgiving foods.

22

What else do you do on Thanksgiving?

Some kids like to watch the Macy's Thanksgiving Day Parade from New York City.

Some people spend their Thanksgiving helping others who are poor or sick. This helps everyone feel better.

Thanksgiving is about more than a big meal.

It is a chance to think about what is good in our lives. These are the things we can be thankful for.

When Thanksgiving comes this year, what will you be thankful for?

29

Words You Know

Thanksgiving

cranberries

harvest

parade

Native Americans

oysters

Pilgrims

turkey

Index

About the Author

David F. Marx is an author and editor of children's books. He resides in the Chicago area.

Photo Credits

Photographs ©: Corbis-Bettmann: 8 (Archivo Iconográfico, S. A.), 11, 15, 31 top right; Liaison Agency, Inc.: 17 top (Eric Horan); Lynn M. Stone: 7, 30 bottom right; PhotoEdit: 25 (Myrleen Ferguson), 18, 31 bottom right (F. Martinez), 29 (Tom McCarthy), 22, 31 top left (A. Ramey), 26 (David Young-Wolff); Stock Boston: 17 bottom, 30 bottom left (Vincent De Witt), 16, 31 center (Raoul Hackel), cover (Dorothy Littlle-Greco); Superstock, Inc.: 12, 21, 31 bottom left; Tony Stone Images: 19 (Art Wolfe), 3, 30 top (David Young-Wolff).